Stone Soup

A Modern Fable

Paul Thain

Samuel French—London
New York-Toronto-Hollywood

FOR AMATEUR PRODUCTION ENQUIRIES

**UNITED KINGDOM AND WORLD
EXCLUDING NORTH AMERICA**
plays@SamuelFrench-London.co.uk
020 7255 4302/01

Each title is subject to availability from Samuel French,

depending upon country of performance.

CHARACTERS

Newsboy
Sophia
Shamir
Camilla
Jason
Ahmed
Doreen
Makomo
Kausu
Hannah
Ti-Sung
Boy
Girl
Man
Woman
Thin Girl
Henry North
Martha North
General Mayhem
Major Hazard
Soldiers
Children

PRODUCTION NOTE

The cooking-pot featured in *Stone Soup* should be huge. A giant papier-mâché construction could be a fun challenge, but a two-dimensional cardboard cut-out will also be fine. Obviously the actors must suggest its massive size and weight as they drag it to its position centre stage.

For my Mother

STONE SOUP

The Village. Afternoon

The ground is littered with stones

The light is bright; as the play progresses it fades to dusk. Cicadas sing in the afternoon heat (a sound which continues throughout the play) as the rich and poor of many nations, as represented by Shamir, Camilla, Ahmed, Doreen, Makomo, Kausu, Hannah, Ti-Sung and others, go about their daily tasks: one sows seed, another ploughs, others march, some squat in the dust slapping chapattis, one argues on a telephone, another studies a computer print-out, and a young woman nurses her starving child. All this is performed through mime, using minimal props. We also hear improvised snatches of different languages, real and imaginary

A Newsboy weaves through the Villagers

Newsboy Read all about it! Read all about it! Man Murders Future! Man Murders Future! Read all about it!

The Newsboy exits at speed

Sophia, an old woman, enters, carrying an exquisitely carved staff. Magic charms hang from her rainbow dress -— chicken bones and ostrich feathers, silver bells and cockle shells. She begins a ritual dance, singing and chanting in a forgotten language. The Villagers back away from her

Sophia Closer, come closer ... What's wrong? Don't you like my little dance? What — not even my wonderful voice? Or perhaps you are afraid? No? You are not afraid? Good — so please, come closer. (*To one of the Villagers*) Yes, you. (*To two other Villagers*) You and you. No, no, no, no — why do you skulk in the shadows? Surely you are not afraid of a harmless old woman? All of you — stop. Stop what you're doing and listen. Listen to my story and I promise you will share my dreams.

Shamir We have no time for dreams, woman. We must work.

Sophia Work? Work for what? More work? Wait, wait! Are you all so blind? Look into my eyes. I am a shaman, a trickster, a priest of Paradise — enter my world, and I will feed your souls.

Camilla Not me soul needs feeding, darling, it's me belly.

The Villagers laugh

Sophia To feed one, my dear, you must feed both. (*She draws a circle on the floor with her staff*) See, I draw the magic circle ... So come, please, gather round, all of you, hear my story. It is an ancient tale heavy with hope and full of fun. It begins when old Mother Earth takes on human form and visits the world of ——

Shamir Listen, you old hag, haven't I told you? We haven't time for stupid stories! We must work! We have to work!

Sophia Work, work, all the time work. Are you a man or a beast? Very well. As you wish. Only before I go at least let me share your hospitality. I haven't eaten for three days.

Ahmed Three days! Some poor wretches here haven't eaten for three weeks!

Doreen That's right, times are hard, so push off; there's nothing for you here.

Camilla You heard. Go on — scram!

Makomo Leave us, woman. Sell your sugared words in another village.

Sophia All I want is a little food.

Shamir I tell you, we have nothing.

Hannah These are dark days ——

Kausu — dying days ——

Makomo — days of plague and famine.
Hannah Rain burns ——
Shamir — fish choke ——
Ahmed — rivers run to dust.
Camilla Crops fail ——
Hannah — children starve ——
Makomo — Generals plead for better bombs.
Ahmed The very air burns our throats ——
Hannah — stings our eyes ——
Camilla — rots our lungs ——
Ahmed Soon this will be a Village of ghosts.
Sophia Stinking sons of Satan! You refuse an old woman! Would you see me starve? Have you no shame? None of you? Not even one? Very well; rot in hell, for all I care! Hunger has hardened your miserable hearts, I shall just have to settle for soup.
Hannah Soup? You have soup and you dare beg from us?
Sophia Not beg, I never beg: I share. Always I share. Ah, but enough, enough. If things are so bad, we should not quarrel. You and I, we must be friends. So, I forgive you, I forgive you all. And, perhaps, I even still share my soup. Yes, why not? Suddenly I feel good. I will share it, all of it, every last drop. I will make soup for us all.
Hannah What? All of us? You can feed us all?
Sophia Have I not said? Now, please, close your silly mouths or instead you will be eating flies! I tell you, in this world all things are possible. Bring me a big enough pot and I will feed the entire Village.
Ahmed All of us?
Sophia Are you gone deaf? I feed everyone, even the poor. That's right, my foolish friends, I even feed the poor. So what are you all waiting for? Quickly, quickly! I need a pot! Run! Run! Find a pot! How can I cook without a pot? Quickly, quickly, before I change my mind! (*She raises her staff*)

There is a crash of thunder

A pot! A pot! I need a pot! A great, big cooking pot!

There is more thunder. Sophia spins the staff high above her head and the Lights flash

Makomo, it is you! I choose you! Run! Run! Run for your people! Run for the hungry! Run for the weak!

Makomo circles Sophia as if attached to her staff by an invisible thread

Run, run, faster and faster...

Makomo's running becomes stylised, going into slow-motion, his breathing becoming deep and heavy

... run, run, faster, faster, faster and faster...

The Lights and sound create pictures of Makomo's journey. He runs through an ancient tropical jungle, with a strange cacophony of animal and bird cries in the background

Africa! The true Eden! Cradle of humanity! Run, Makomo! North! Run north! Follow the star and run like the wind!

Makomo leaves the tropical jungle; the Lights and sound change and he enters the city, where there are sounds of traffic and screaming sirens

Hear the hate, see the pain, feel the anger burn your brain. Let the concrete pound your feet, so that soon we all can eat!
Newsboy (*unseen*) Read all about it! Man Murders Future! Read all about it!
Sophia A pot, a pot, I need a pot, a great, big cooking pot!

Makomo stops and rings a mimed, but audible, doorbell. He waits, head lowered, panting hard

Sophia observes from the shadows as:

Henry North, an Englishman in his fifties, enters and opens the (mimed) door

Henry Makomo! My dear fellow — what a surprise! How nice to see you!
Makomo Please, please, Mr North ——
Henry Whatever is it, old chap?
Makomo I beg you. We need — we need to borrow the pot.
Henry Pot, pot? What pot?
Makomo The cooking pot, the giant cooking pot.
Henry The giant cooking pot? Don't be ridiculous, you've nothing to put in it. You can't possibly need one that big!
Makomo No, no, a woman, an old woman; she has promised to feed us all, everyone, the entire Village.
Henry Everyone?
Makomo Even the poor.
Henry Good lord ...
Makomo Isn't it wonderful?
Henry Well, yes, absolutely. But feed the poor? How can she possibly ——
Makomo Soup. She promises to make soup for us all. But, of course, as you well know, our pot is extremely small.
Henry Ah, yes, right, I see ... Yes, well you'd better come in then.

He mimes closing the door

Makomo Thank you.
Henry The whole Village, eh? Well, that's certainly a turn-up. Fantastic!

A clock delicately tinkles the eleventh hour

Of course we — er — we had hoped to help you ourselves, but, well, you know, what with one thing and a ——

The voice of Martha North, an American in her forties, comes from off stage

Martha (*off*) Henry ...
Henry (*whispering*) God's sake — wipe your feet.
Martha (*off*) Henry, who is it?
Henry (*calling to Martha*) It's all right, darling — only Makomo.
(*To Makomo*) Quick, the pot's through here.

Henry and Makomo begin to tiptoe towards the exit. As they do so ...

Martha enters

Martha Makomo! Oh, my dear, how nice of you to visit us!
Makomo Mrs North ——

Martha and Makomo embrace

Martha (*to Makomo*) Mmm — aren't you a darling?(*To Henry*)
Isn't he a darling, darling?
Henry Yes, darling.
Martha Always so kind ——
Henry — so obliging ——
Martha — so helpful ——
Henry — so patient ——
Martha (*to Makomo*) So, what have you brought us today, hmm?
Something real special, I bet?
Makomo Mrs North ——
Martha Something real scrumptious and tasty, hmm?
Makomo Mrs North ——
Martha God, am I hungry! Makomo, I tell you right now I could kill
for a hamburger! I could, I could, I really could. Or maybe, maybe
a steak, a succulent, tender ——
Makomo Mrs North ——
Martha — or perhaps even a nice, juicy ——
Makomo Mrs North, please, this is not why I have come.
Martha It's not? So why the hell have you ——?
Henry Darling, he hasn't brought food, he's here to ——
Martha No food? Hasn't brought food?
Henry He's here to borrow the ——

Martha What do you mean, he hasn't brought food? Goddamnit! He owes us! Hey, wait a minute, I get it — this is some sick joke, right? What the hell is this? Wind-up Martha time?

Makomo Mrs North, forgive me, but I can bring you no more food. We cannot even feed ourselves.

Martha So what's new? Don't give me that. You think we don't have problems? You think we don't have plenty hungry and homeless? A deal's a deal, Makomo, and you people owe us a whole heap of money. So either you pay us back with food, or else I send in the boys to kick ass. Starting with yours. OK? Savvy?

Henry I think what my wife — what my wife means ——

Martha Shut it, Henry.

Henry But darling, there's no need to be quite so ——

Martha I said shut it. (*To Makomo*) Aw, Makomo, hey, come on, why so sad? These are hard times for everybody. Hell, do you realize, I personally, myself personally, haven't eaten a bite since breakfast?

Henry But darling, that's what I'm trying to tell you: we're all going to have soup. That's why ——

Martha Soup?

Henry Yes, darling, the whole Village — everyone.

Martha Soup!

Henry Isn't it marvellous?

Martha I don't want goddamn soup! I want hamburger!

During the following, Henry and Makomo start to tiptoe away

Hamburger with french fries, lots of french fries, and onion, and ketchup, and pickle and ... and where the hell do you think you're going?

Henry To — er — to help Makomo with the pot, dearest.

Martha The hell you are!

Henry Martha, be reasonable: no pot, no soup.

Martha Got it in one, Henry; seems like we have ourselves a monopoly situation here. Not that we'd ever take advantage, oh no. This is just honest to goodness free trade. So tell me, Makomo, without seeming, you know, too blunt: what's in it for us?

Makomo You will have a share of the soup.

Martha Damn right. So how big a share?

Makomo A fair share — the same as everyone else.

Martha (*laughing*)The same as everyone else? Do you hear that, Henry? Now what kind of goddamn commie talk is that, Makomo? Everyone else don't have a cooking pot, now do they?

Makomo You would profit from starving people?

Martha Hey, easy, easy; let's not get sentimental here. You prefer we insult you with charity? Ah, come on, you think I don't feel bad about this? Hey, we're friends, right? Normally you could have it, of course you could, no question. But like I say, these are difficult times.

Henry We're all up against it, old chum. Believe me, it's dog eat dog.

Martha That's right. So let's cut the crap and start again for real, shall we?

Henry After all, old man, it is our pot. And as much as we sympathize ——

Martha Henry?

Henry Yes, darling?

Martha Shut up.

Henry Sorry, darling.

Martha OK, my friend— so what's the deal, hmm?

Makomo looks thoughtful. A drum begins to beat

Well, Makomo? Exactly how big a share?

The drumbeats build to a climax

Black-out

We hear more drumbeats and African-style cries of celebration

The Lights come up on the Village square. A pile of wood has been assembled

Makomo enters, returning with the pot (which contains a large ladle) surrounded by the excited villagers (except Doreen and Camilla) and Sophia

Sophia Well done, Makomo, this is a fine pot. With such a pot I can feed us all.
Makomo Woman, this soup had better be good. They bargained hard; I had to sell my children's future.

The Villagers surround the pot with kindling. Sophia sits on a rock

Sophia Ah, don't worry. My soup, it is the food of the gods! With their blessing your children will be giants! But first we must have fire. Come, more wood! Bring more wood! More wood! More wood! Bring me more wood!

Camilla and Doreen approach, dragging wood

Camilla All right, all right ...
Doreen Hold your horses ...
Camilla (*referring to Sophia*) It's all right for her ——-
Doreen — sitting on her lazy bum ——
Camilla We've trudged ten miles of hot sand carrying this lot.
Doreen Five miles there, five miles back ——
Camilla — each day a little further ——
Doreen — each day harder to find ——
Sophia More wood! More wood!
Doreen Steady on, it don't grow on trees.
Camilla Not any more.
Sophia Feed the flames! Feast the fire!

The fire roars and crackles into life. The fire is represented by cardboard cut-out tongues of flame

Doreen She don't half go on.
Sophia Burn! Burn!
Camilla Bit weird if you ask me.
Sophia That's it! That's better! Burn! Burn! I want it hotter than hell!

The Villagers place the pot in the fire

Doreen So when's this soup gonna be ready then?
Sophia Patience, my friends, soon you will have your reward.

*As the water boils and bubbles, some of the crowd of villagers
provide an orchestrated refrain of appropriate sound effects. This
will be a recurring set piece, silly and fun*

Villagers Bloop, bloop, bloop ... Bloop, bloop, bloop, bloop ...Bloop,
    bloop ... Bloop ... Bloop, bloop ...
Sophia See how it boils and bubbles. Already the miracle begins.
    I use an ancient recipe: fire, water, earth and air ——
Doreen Earth?
Sophia My God! How stupid! Yes, you're right — I use no earth!
    How can even I make stone soup without earth?
Makomo What soup?
Camilla Stone soup?
Doreen What did she say?
Ahmed (*to Sophia*) What did you say?
Sophia Stone soup.
Makomo Stone soup?
Sophia My favourite.
Hannah You mean soup ... soup made with — with stones?
Sophia But of course! How else?
Camilla Stones? Stones?
Makomo What cruel joke is this?
Doreen She's mad!
Camilla A nutter! A bloody nutter! A stark, raving ——
Sophia No, no, no — it is delicious. I promise you will all love it.
Shamir You crazy, crazy bitch, the sun has boiled your brain.
Sophia I tell you, it is the finest food in the world!
Hannah Stupid, stupid woman. Can you not see? Look at me; I am
    starving. My children are starving. You promise — you promised
    us all food. And because you promise, I promise my children.
Ahmed You expect us to feed them stone soup?
Sophia Why not? Children — all children — they love my soup!
Doreen Silly old cow.
Shamir I tell you, she is mad.

Sophia Trust me, my friends — all will be well. My soup, it will nourish their hearts and feast their souls!

Makomo You would give a starving child a stone? Dear God, it is all too, too sad.

Hannah The spirits have sent her to mock our misery ...

Camilla Yeah, I like a nice drop of soup, an' all.

Doreen Yeah, me too.

Hannah What fools we are.

Makomo Woman, you were my last hope.

Sophia Then believe. Look into my eyes. These are days of miracle and wonder. Even as I speak, a new world is struggling to be born. It is the beginning of a new age. So please — trust me. All of you — I want you all to bring me a stone, a nice round juicy stone. Well, why do you stand like lost sheep? I need stones. How can I cook without stones? Please, a little faith, hm? A few stones, that's all. What have you got to lose?

Ahmed (*picking up a stone and handing it to Sophia*) Very well. Here, woman — here is my stone.

Sophia Oh, yes. And very nice too.

Ahmed Now let me see you eat it.

Sophia Eat it?

Ahmed That's right — eat it.

Sophia You are a wise man — you have chosen well. This is a good stone, a very good stone. This kind, you know, it is particularly succulent.

Ahmed Then eat it.

Sophia (*sniffing the stone*) Mmm ... smell ... So full of flavour, yes? Almost like truffle ...

Ahmed So eat it.

Sophia No, no, no, it would not be right.

Ahmed You crazy woman, I want to see you eat it!

Sophia But my dear friend, remember: always I prefer to share.

Ahmed Eat it! Eat it! Eat it, I say! Eat it! Eat it, damn you!

Sophia All right, all right, no need to bite off my head. I will eat the stone, relax, no problem. Only first, of course, it must be cooked ... (*She drops the stone into the pot*)

Boy (*as the stone falls into the pot*) Plop.

Sophia Excellent. Now, who's next? That's right, don't be shy.

The Children pick up stones and rush to the pot

Children Here ... mine ... mine ... take mine ...
Sophia Thank you, thank you, my beautiful children. Well done; thank you, thank you ...

The Villagers and Sophia put the stones into the pot in time to the following sounds

Girl Plop, plop.
Sophia Such delicious, juicy stones ...
Man Plop.
Sophia Thank you, thank you ... oh, yes, very nice ...
Woman Plop, plop, plop.
Sophia (*taking a stone from Shamir*) No, no, no, Shamir — this one, it is not so good. Smell. You see — not so fresh. Yes, yes, that one; that one is better.
Boy Pl ... op ...
Sophia Ah, now this — this indeed is a stone among stones! See! My God! What colour! Such fragrance! Already my mouth it waters.
Woman Plop, plop.
Sophia More stones, more stones.
Villagers Plop, bloop ... plop, plop, bloop ... plop, bloop, plop, plop, bloop ... plop, plop, bloop ... plop ... pl ... op ...
Sophia Excellent, excellent.
Villagers Bloop, bloop, bloop ... Bloop, bloop, bloop, bloop ...

More Children approach the pot

Second Boy Is it true? Is it really true?
Second Girl Is it? Can you feed us? Can you feed us all?
Third Boy They say you can feed us all.
Third Girl All of us, even the poor, even the most poor.
Second Girl Can you? Can you really?

Sophia I will try; I will surely try.
Children When? When? When?
Sophia Soon. Soon, I hope. Very soon. Only first, first I must boil the stones to bring out their full flavour. Perhaps one of you would like to help me stir?
Children Me! Me! Me!

The Children laugh and giggle as they help stir the contents of the giant pot using Sophia's staff

Sophia Now, now, don't push, don't push. Yes, all right — you. You first. That's right, nice and gentle, a good gentle stir. And now you — you next. Good, very good..
Villagers Bloop, bloop, bloop ... Bloop, bloop, bloop, bloop ... Bloop, bloop, bloop ...
Sophia Good, very good; so let me take a little taste, eh? (*She takes a noisy sip*) Mmm — wonderful! Wonderful!

The Children cheer

Villagers Bloop, bloop, bloop ... Bloop, bloop, bloop, bloop ... Bloop, bloop, bloop ...
Ahmed (*sniffing the air*) You know something, my belly, it aches so much, I think I can actually smell this soup!
Doreen Yeah, I know what you mean.
Makomo I tell you, that crazy woman has charmed us all.
Camilla Be nice, though, wouldn't it? I can almost smell it meself. Famished, I am.
Doreen You an' me both, love. Mind you, talk about grasping at straws.
Camilla Stone soup, eh? Stroll on!

Everyone but Sophia chuckles

Dear, oh dear ...
Doreen I don't know — if we didn't laugh, we'd cry, eh?
Camilla What is the world coming to, though, eh?

Doreen Funny old world, all right.
Camilla Diabolical.
Makomo Out of balance.
Camilla Top-heavy——
Makomo — upside-down ——
Doreen — helter-skelter——
Camilla — topsy-turvy.
Doreen Not so bad for you, mind; you're used to being hungry and
    homeless. We're not.
Villagers Bloop, bloop, bloop ... Bloop, bloop, bloop, bloop ...
    Bloop, bloop, bloop ...
Sophia (*taking a disgustingly noisy sip*) Ah ... I do so like a tasty
    stone soup! (*She sips again*) Ah, delicious! But listen, I tell you
    a secret; stone soup, stone soup with cabbage, now that is even
    better, that is really hard to beat!
Camilla Stone soup with cabbage! Ooh, that sounds nice.
Ahmed Anything. Anything would be nice.
Camilla Yes ... sounds very nice, that does. Doesn't it, Doreen?
Doreen Shh, quiet.
Camilla Very nice indeed.
Sophia Ah, yes, stone soup.
Camilla (*to Doreen*) Don't you think? Hint, hint.
Sophia Stone soup with cabbage ...
Doreen (*to Camilla*) Don't you dare — I'm saving them.
Camilla What? All of them?
Doreen Quiet, will you! They're all I've got.
Sophia What a delight!
Camilla (*to Doreen*) Go on.
Sophia I remember it well.
Camilla (*to Doreen*)You won't miss one.
Sophia So strong ——
Camilla (*to Doreen*) Go on ——
Doreen Oh, well, all right, I suppose.
Sophia Ah, but what a taste! Such a taste! How can mere
    words ——
Doreen (*to Sophia*)I've — er — I've got a cabbage.

Sophia A cabbage? You have a cabbage? A whole cabbage? But this — this is wonderful!

Doreen Well, it's only a scrawny little ——

Sophia No matter, no matter, hurry, hurry, I'm sure it will be most splendid!

Doreen (*heading for the exit*)All right then, shan't be long.

Sophia Oh, and a little salt, perhaps? To enhance the flavour ...

Doreen Salt? I ain't got no salt.

Doreen exits: she returns during the following dialogue with a cabbage, which she puts into the pot

Ahmed I have salt. I can bring salt.

Ahmed exits, returning during the following dialogue with salt, which he puts into the pot

Sophia Excellent, excellent; soon, my friends, I swear we shall feast like kings! (*She hums happily*)

The Lights focus on the pot. Sophia "la - la's" the tune of the Ode to Joy from Beethoven's Ninth Symphony and the Villagers join in, "blooping" the tune. The song reaches a crescendo

A small, ragged Thin Girl approaches the pot, holding a bowl

Thin Girl Please, is it ready yet?

Sophia My dear, I am sorry but you must be patient. No, no, wait. Perhaps you would like to help me stir?

Thin Girl Thank you, but I cannot stay.

The Thin Girl lowers her head sadly and moves away

Boy (*to Sophia*) I will! I'll help.

Sophia Why, thank you, my child. That's right, a good stir, give it a good stir. And now, now let me take another little sip. (*She slurps* *the soup noisily*) Mmmm! Ah! Joy of joys! Delicious! That is so, so good! Although, mind you, to be perfectly, absolutely and totally honest, stone soup, stone soup with turnip — now that is also very, very good.

Child Turnip? I know where there's a turnip.

Sophia You do? Bless you, my sweet child! Quickly, quickly, go get it! Tonight I swear you will sleep without hunger.

The Child runs off, returning during the following dialogue with a turnip, which is added to the pot

(*Taking another noisy slurp*)Ah, so rich, so much flavour! All the time it improves! I tell you: stone soup, it is the finest food in the world! Mind you, I did once have stone soup with carrots ... Oh, my God, now there's a delight!

Hannah Stone soup with carrots?

Sophia You have some, perhaps?

Hannah Me? No, no, forgive me, please, but I have nothing.

Sophia Nothing? What? Nothing at all?

Hannah Nothing. No work, no home, no husband, nothing; my whole life, it has been worth nothing. Each day I struggle to feed my children. But each day they grow more weak and cry for life. And I cannot help them. How can I? There is no work, I have no land — all I can do is beg and steal. But it is still not enough. Soon my children will waste into ghosts. And yet, yet I know there are those in this Village who have food, plenty food. There is a man here who has a whole mountain of carrots ——

Kausu My carrots are to be sold, they are not for free.

Hannah I would pay if I could, only you are so drunk with greed you would rather die than lower your price.

Kausu Ignorant woman, what can you understand of economics?

Hannah My children are dying. What is there to understand? Are you deaf to their cries? A few carrots: what is that to you?

Kausu If I don't protect my profit, I too will starve.

Hannah And how do you protect my children?

Kausu I have my own troubles. Your children are not my concern.

Sophia Oh, dear, dear, what a foolish, greedy man you are! Don't you realise, stone soup with carrots is a rare delight never to be missed. But if you deny us, you must also deny yourself. Is that what you want? Hm? Well? Is it?

Kausu (*licking his lips and sighing*) Stone soup with carrots — it really is that good, eh?

Sophia Good? Good? Is it good? Listen, my fat, foolish friend: bring me carrots and you will have a taste of Paradise.

Kausu exits and fetches carrots during the following

Villagers Bloop, bloop, bloop ... Bloop, bloop, bloop, bloop ... Bloop, bloop, bloop ...

Makomo You know, perhaps Ahmed was not so crazy. I myself can smell this stone soup. And, do you know, it smells rather good.

Sophia Oh, you think so, do you? Well, what do you know, eh? Ha! I tell you this is nothing, nothing! I remember once I made stone soup with a little salt beef. Ah! Now that — that was magnificent! Truly magnificent!

Jason My Mum's got some sa ——

Camilla slaps Jason

Ow! What was that for?

Everyone looks at Camilla

Camilla Why are you all staring? Don't look at me like — well, all right, what if I have? It's only a tiny little ——

Jason No, it's ——

Camilla slaps him again

Ow!

Sophia tuts. All eyes remain fixed on Camilla

Doreen You've got salt beef?
Camilla Doreen, it's miniscule. Microscopic. Tiny. Hardly worth
   the ——
Doreen You had my bleedin' cabbage quick enough!
Camilla Honest, love, it wouldn't ——
Doreen Honest? Honest! I'm surprised you don't choke! You told
   me you had nothin'! You rotten, two-faced ——
Camilla Here! Who you calling ——
Doreen I'll tell you who I'm calling ——
Camilla Oh, you will, will you?
Doreen Yes, I will.
Camilla Oh yeah?
Doreen Yeah!

Camilla and Doreen begin to wrestle

Sophia Ladies, please, please!
Camilla I'll kill her, I will — I will, I'll — ow!
Doreen Serves you right!
Sophia Oh, dear, dear, dear —— (*She raises her staff*)

*The Lights flash and a crash of thunder is heard. Doreen and
Camilla immediately stop fighting and look up at the sky, astonished*

   Have you learned nothing? We should not fight, we must help one
   another

There is a pause. Doreen and Camilla look chastened

Doreen (*to Camilla*) Well? You heard. So what's it to be?
Camilla Oh, all right then. (*She moves to exit*) Only God knows
   what my Fred'll say.

Camilla exits to fetch the salt beef during the following

Doreen (*calling off*) Oh, and bring some garlic. I like garlic. An'
   don't say you've got none 'cos I know you have!

Villagers Bloop, bloop, bloop, ... Bloop, bloop, bloop, bloop ... Bloop, bloop, bloop ...

Sophia stirs the soup. The Thin Girl approaches the pot

Sophia You again.
Thin Girl Please, is it ready yet?
Sophia No, my child. I'm sorry, but you must be patient.

The girl turns away sadly

Villagers Bloop, bloop, bloop, ... Bloop, bloop, bloop, bloop ... Bloop, bloop, bloop ...

Ti-Sung helps to stir the contents of the pot

Bloop, bloop, bloop, ... Bloop, bloop, bloop, bloop ... Bloop, bloop, bloop ...
Ti-Sung My father was a brave man; I think you would have liked him. Many times he risked his life calling for justice. Even when they put him in prison, he wouldn't stay silent. The last time I saw him, not long before they killed him, he told me — he told me if I dream of a better world I help to make it real. Do you believe that? Do you think it can be true?
Sophia Of course it's true. We are in the world and the world is in us. The world, it is made of dreams, many, many dreams, each a possible future, each future struggling to shape reality. If we let them, the bad dreams, the greedy dreams will eat us all up. But the good ones — the good dreams, they are hungry for change, and if we are wise they will nourish our world with peace and plenty.
Ti-Sung But how can we tell the good dreams from the bad?
Sophia Ah, it is not so difficult. That which brings us together is good. That which divides us is bad. What could be more simple? Now listen, come closer, listen to the pot. Well? Do you hear? Can you hear?

The Villagers "bloop" to the tune of Bach's "Jesu, Joy of Man's Desiring", Sophia conducting with her staff. Ti-Sung nods and

*smiles. As this interlude ends, the Thin Girl approaches the pot
again*

Thin Girl Please, is it ready yet?
Sophia Haven't I told you? Haven't I said? Why can't you wait like
  the rest?

The Girl turns sadly away

  I'm sorry, my child, but you must be patient.

*Henry and Martha enter in a comic car, tooting the horn loudly;
the car backfires and gives off lots of smoke*

Henry Well, hallo there.
Martha Hi.
Sophia Mr and Mrs North.

*Henry and Martha eagerly make for the pot. Martha stares into the
pot and sniffs*

Henry (*to Sophia and the Villagers*) No, no, please, no need for
  ceremony — just happened to be passing.
Martha Mmmm — smells wonderful!
Henry (*to Martha*) Weren't we darling? Darling?
Martha Hmm? Oh. Yes, that's right—just passing. You know, just
  passing by ——
Henry Thought we'd drop in ——
Martha See how all you good people are getting on.
Sophia You are most welcome!

Sophia, Martha and Henry stand awkwardly, exchanging smiles

Henry To be perfectly honest, we couldn't resist the soup, could we,
  darling?
Martha I don't suppose you do hamburgers.

Sophia Hamburgers? What? Cow in a bun? No, no, no, cows in buns, they cost the earth; I make soup, stone soup.

Henry What soup?

Sophia Stone soup.

Henry You mean soup made with — with ——?

Sophia Stones; nice, fresh, juicy stones.

Martha Stones?

Sophia These are, of course, special stones.

Henry Ah, yes, I see.

Martha Well, I'm damned if I do.

Sophia It is an ancient peasant recipe.

Henry Amazing. Now isn't that amazing, darling, absolutely amazing? Stone soup, eh? Splendid! Now if that's not being resourceful, I don't know what is. Nothing like adversity to bring out the old native genius, eh?

Martha Soup made with stones? But — but how? It smells so good.

Henry Yes, well ... These peasant people, you see, darling, sons of the soil. Certainly know their onions when they get in a pickle, ha-ha. I remember once in Tuscany ——

Martha Henry, please, you're giving me a migraine. Oh, excuse me, I feel quite — quite faint.

Sophia Oh, my poor dear!

Martha Don't you worry about me, I'll — I'll be all right.

Henry Darling, are you sure?

Martha It's probably just, you know — hunger.

Henry But darling — you've only just had lunch.

Martha Henry?

Henry Yes, darling?

Martha Shut up.

Henry Yes, darling. Sorry, darling.

Martha (*wobbling*) Oh, no, no, don't worry, I'll — I'll be fine. Probably.

Sophia Well, my soup, it is not quite ready yet, but would you like a little taste?

Martha Does a duck like water? (*She quickly recovers, seizes the ladle and takes a big, noisy slurp*) Oh, my dear ... (*She slurps again*) My dear, it's wonderful!

The Villagers nod and murmur appreciatively. Martha has another slurp

Henry Darling, do you ... do you think I might, might possibly ...?
Martha (*taking another slurp of the soup*) My God ... Oh, my God ... (*She slurps again*)
Henry Darling ... ?
Martha Do be quiet, Henry. (*She takes another slurp*) Mmm — this is so good. (*And another*)
Sophia Perhaps Mr North might also like to taste —— ?
Martha Excuse me? Oh, I'm sorry! Oh, my manners — what must you think! (*She hands the ladle to Henry*) Here, Henry, now don't you dare be greedy!
Henry Thank you, darling. (*He slurps the soup*) Oh, I say, now that is good.
Sophia Ah — you are too kind. But here ... let me try ... (*She takes the ladle and slurps the soup*) Ah, no, no, no, no ... it is still not right.
Martha You mean — you mean it could be even better ——?
Sophia Well, as we know, only God is perfect. But I tell you something, just between ourselves: stone soup, stone soup with chicken, ah, now that — that is almost sacrilege!
Martha That means it's good, right?
Sophia Good? I tell you it is ambrosia!
Henry It does sound rather special. So, all we — all we need is a chicken, eh? Do we, er — do we happen to know anyone who might possibly have a chicken, dearest?
Martha Henry, I think we've contributed quite enough already!
Henry Ah, yes: the pot. Yes, indeed. It is our pot, you see. On hire.
Martha And on the most generous of terms. Not that we ever get any thanks. Oh, no. Why is it always us, eh? Why can't someone else bring a goddamn chicken?
Sophia These people are poor, only you have chicken.
Martha Is that so? Well, that's just too bad.
Henry Oh. Oh dear.
Sophia Dear, oh dear ...

Henry What a pity.

Sophia Yes, a pity, a great pity, a great, great pity, a great, great, great pity — what a pity, such a pity .

Henry Stone soup with chicken, eh? Must be quite something ...

Sophia Oh, yes. Yes, indeed. Indeed it is.

Henry (*nodding, and licking his lips*) Let's suppose, let's just suppose we did have one ...

Sophia What? A chicken!

Martha Henry! Don't you dare!

Sophia You have a chicken?

Henry Now, now, I didn't actually say ——

Sophia Listen, everyone: this man from the North, he has a chicken!

There is a huge cheer from the Villagers

Martha Henry, I hope you know what you're doing.

Henry Darling, I understand these people. Diplomacy, clear, concise thinking, that's what we need. All right, everyone, quiet please! Quiet! Quiet, now! Thank you. Thank you very much. Good, excellent. Splendid. Now, let's get down to -- er — to — er — oh, dear, where, where exactly was I?

Sophia Chicken. Stone soup with chicken.

Henry Ah, yes, yes. Ah, but, er — no, no, no.

Sophia No, no, no?

Henry No, no, no — not chicken. Hypothetical chicken.

Sophia Hypo — what — ical?

Henry Let us suppose, let us just suppose, hypothetically, simply for the purposes of speculation and conjecture, that we did indeed have a chicken ——

Sophia Is this a real chicken? Or a hypothetical chicken?

Henry A real chicken. Hypothetically.

Sophia A real, hypothetical chicken, I see.

Henry You do? Excellent. Well ... ?

Sophia Well, what?

Henry Well, supposing we did, supposing we did have one: what would be your position? I mean, could we — could we reach some kind of understanding?

Sophia What? With the chicken?

Henry No, no, no, not the chicken — you and I. Between you and
I.

Sophia What kind of understanding?

Henry Well, since Mrs North and I have already been most
generous *vis-à-vis* the cooking pot, I think in the circumstances,
taking everything into account, and paying proper and due regard
to all extenuating economic circumstances, it would be only
reasonable for you to procure, or rather acquire, that is to say
purchase outright exclusively and entirely all benefits and liabili-
ties pertaining to said chicken.

Sophia You mean you want us to buy it?

Henry Precisely.

Sophia But how? We have no money.

Henry My dear lady, no problem: we simply arrange credit. Eat
now, pay later. Simple. Pay us whatever you like ——

Sophia Mr North ——

Henry — any old cash crop'll do ... cotton, tobacco ——

Sophia Mr North ——

Henry — roses. Yes, even roses; there's always a good demand
for ——

Sophia Mr North, please understand: either we all eat stone soup
with chicken, or none of us does.

Henry I say, that's a bit extreme.

Sophia All or none, that is how it must be.

Henry I don't think I like your tone.

Sophia Then you don't like the truth; deny us, and you deny
yourselves. There is no other way.

Henry Yes, there is. Suppose we had two pots.

Sophia Two pots?

Henry One for us and one for the — for the others.

Sophia Mr North ——

Henry Equal but different.

Sophia No, Mr North.

Henry Very well, all right, what if we were to ——?

Sophia No! I have said no!

Henry You might at least have the common courtesy ——

Sophia No, no, no! One world, one people, one pot!
Villagers One world, one people, one pot!
Sophia That is how it must be. And if you don't like it, you can take your chicken and stuff it!
Henry Well, really!

Sophia ignores him, stirring the soup, her anger echoed by the Villagers

Villagers Bloop, bloop, bloop, bloop ... Bloop, bloop, bloop, bloop ... Bloop, bloop, bloop, bloop ...

The Thin Girl approaches again

Thin Girl Please ...
Sophia Yes, my dear, what is it? Oh, it's you again.
Thin Girl Please, is it ready yet?
Sophia Haven't I told you a hundred times? Eh? Haven't I? You must be patient and you must wait! You must wait like the rest!
Thin Girl But it's for my brother. He's dying. I don't think he can wait.
Sophia (*kneeling and holding the Thin Girl*) My dear child, forgive me; I've done all I can, there is nothing more I can do. But tell your brother, tell him to hold on to his life, to hold very tight because soon, soon my soup it will be ready, and I promise, I promise, he will be the first.
Thin Girl (*sadly turning away*) Thank you.

Martha sniffs. Henry comforts her, dabbing her eyes

Henry Didn't I tell you? Didn't I say we shouldn't come? All this suffering. You know how it upsets you.
Martha Henry ...
Henry Yes, darling?
Martha Go get the chicken.

The Villagers give a huge cheer. Henry hugs Martha

The Lights change to a tight focus on the pot. There is another bloop interlude, another tightly orchestrated set piece:

Villagers Bloop, bloop, bloop, bloop, bloop ...
Woman Plop, plop ...
Man Bloop, bloop ...

Sophia smiles and, swaying rhythmically, begins to conduct the Villagers

Villagers Bloop, bloop, bloop, bloop, bloop ...
Girl Plop, plop ...
Boy Bloop, bloop ...

The Villagers repeat the above; harmony begins to emerge and gradually we begin to discern Strauss' "Blue Danube"

Sophia conducts histrionically; as the piece moves to its climax she dances a flamboyant waltz round and round the pot using the staff as her partner

There is a gunshot. The Villagers scream and panic

Villagers General Mayhem! General Mayhem!

General Mayhem enters, leading Major Hazard and two or three soldiers. The General sports a ridiculous false moustache and is firing a pistol into the air

General Back! Stand back! Out of my way! Move! Move, you
  bloody trash! (*To Ahmed*) Out of my way, you stinking peasant!
Ahmed General Mayhem, please, I beg you ——
General (*striking Ahmed*) You dare address me! On your knees,
  dog! (*To the Soldiers, referring to Sophia*) Right, you, you and
  you — arrest that woman!

There is uproar among the Villagers

Sophia Arrest? Arrest me? But why?

General Hold your tongue, you disgusting old hag! Don't you play the innocent with me! I might be a fool, but I'm not an idiot! You are a dangerous subversive!

Sophia Subversive! But all I do is cook a pot of soup. Is that so terrible?

The Villagers murmur agreement and support

General Silence! I said silence! (*He fires his pistol into the air*)

There is silence

(*Smiling*) Thank you. (*He confronts Sophia*) What kind of fool do you think I am?

Sophia How should I know? There are so many kinds. But you seem to be the worst — the clever kind.

General That's right, bitch — the clever kind, the selfish kind, the kind that might crack your neck if you lie to me again.

Sophia OK, OK, I confess. So while I cook I stir a few thoughts and serve an ancient hope — one world, one people, one pot ...

Villagers One world, one people, one pot ...

General (*firing his pistol*) Silence!

Sophia How else are we to digest a simple truth in a world full of hate and fear? But if you understand this, why should you want to arrest me?

General (*chuckling*) Are you blind? Don't you recognize me? Not even my magnificent moustache? Woman, you see before you General Mayhem, Leader of the Light, Glorious Guardian of the Faith and Protector of the People. All hail!

There is silence

General (*firing his pistol into the air*) I said — all hail!

Villagers (*reluctantly*) All hail ...

General You see? See how they love me? And do you know why? Why they love me? It is because I love them. All of them! I love them all! Individually, they are weak and they stink, and I hate and despise them. But together, together when I bind them into one nation, they are magnificent! The greatest nation in the world! And I, General Mayhem, I am their leader, feeding on hate and feasting on fear, loving humanity and loathing people. Now do you know me?

Sophia Yes, I know you.

General Then you will understand why I cannot allow you to waste this wonderful soup on the weak and the poor.

Sophia The soup is my gift to everyone!

The Villagers cheer

General (*chuckling sardonically*) Everyone? The soup is for everyone! Well, isn't that nice? Hm? Isn't that so generous, so noble and so stupid. Listen, you old hag, are you really that crazy? If you feed them one day, they'll expect to eat every day. Perhaps even twice a day! And how can that be when food is so scarce?

Sophia Food is not so scarce. What is scarce is justice.

Villagers One world, one people, one pot!

The Villagers cheer

General (*firing his pistol*) Justice! So you wish for justice?

Sophia Mock all you like; it is coming. It will happen.

General Only in your dreams, woman. You might as well wish for the sun to freeze.

Sophia It will happen. And it will happen soon. Food, water, shelter; that is the beginning. Basic rights. Basic human rights for everyone. That is what I dream. Because without such rights there can be no true civilization. And without that, people like you will always lead foolish men into waves of blood. (*She prods the General's fat belly*) Now if you will please excuse me, these people are hungry, and it is time to serve my soup ...

General Not so fast! Back! Back! Back you stinking heaps! Quiet! All of you! Listen! There is to be an announcement! An important announcement!

He fires his pistol again. There is silence

Major Hazard!
Major (*stepping forward and stamping on the General's foot*) Sah!
   (*He salutes forcefully, poking himself in the eye*)

The Villagers laugh

The Major moves to stand behind the General

General Quiet! I said quiet! (*He fires his pistol again*)

The Villagers fall silent

Better. That's better. Major Hazard! Major —— (*He steps back,
bumping into the Major*) Ah, there you are! Well, man, what are
you waiting for?

The Major steps forward, holding an unrolled scroll

Major (*reading*) By order —— (*The scroll rolls up suddenly*)
   Sorry, Sah!
General Get on with it!
Major (*reading*) By Order of Our Most ——
General Speak up! Speak up!
Major (*reading: falsetto*) By Order of Our Most Glorious ——
General No, no, not like that, you imbecile! Now get it right, or I
   shall put a hole in your head!
Major (*reading*) By Order of Our Most Glorious Leader ——

The General fires his pistol

Villagers (*mumbling*) All hail ...
General See how they love me? Well, get on with it!
Major (*reading*) This soup — this soup is now under the protection
   of the Ministry of Progress. The aforementioned soup will
   therefore be taken to a place of safety ——

There is uproar from the Villagers

— where the relevant authorities will determine a fair and equitable system of distribution, having given all proper and due regard to race, rank, religion and gender. I thank you.
General You heard: take it away!

There is more uproar

Sophia (*advancing on the General, staff in hand*) Don't you dare! Back! Get back! Ha! You don't frighten me! Touch one drop of this soup and I swear you'll be sorry!
General I warn you, woman: let me have that soup or I will rip your stupid tongue from its root!
Sophia Never! Never, do you hear! One world, one people, one pot!
Villagers One world, one people, one pot!
Sophia One world, one people, one pot!
Villagers One world, one people, one pot!
General Major Hazard!
Major (*jerking to attention*) Sah! (*He again stamps on the General's foot*)
General Ah!
Major Sorry, sir!

Sophia and the Villagers laugh and applaud

Sophia Bravo! Bravo!
General Arrest that woman!
Major Sah! Company — attention!
Henry (*coming forward*) I say, now look here, old man ...
General Mr North! What a delightful surprise! We don't often see you in these parts!
Martha (*approaching the General; to Henry*) Henry, I thought we agreed not to interfere!
General And Mrs North! This is indeed a rare pleasure!
Martha Yes, I'm sure ...

General You're just in time to see me sort a spot of bother with these naughty natives!
Henry Well, actually, that's what I ——
Martha Henry, we must not interfere!
Henry Do excuse us, General. (*To Martha, whispering*) Martha, the man's a monster, an absolute brute.
Martha OK, so he's a son-of-a-bitch, but at least he's *our* son-of-a-bitch.
Henry But how can we be sure? And what about the soup?
Martha Don't you worry, I can handle him. Besides, I feel sure General Mayhem is a man open to reason. Now isn't that right, General? You're not really a monster, are you?
General A monster? Me? Do I look like a monster?
Martha (*to Henry*) You see, Henry: he's really just a big, old softie. (*To the General*) My husband is somewhat concerned about how we deal with the soup, but I've assured him you're a reasonable man.
General Oh, indeed, indeed, I am!
Martha Then I feel confident we can reach some kind of mutually beneficial arrangement.
Henry Martha! Really ...
Sophia You can plot and scheme all you like; my soup is not for you or the General, it is for everyone!

The Villagers cheer

Villagers One world, one people, one pot!
General See how she poisons their minds?
Sophia You have no honour; I'm not afraid of you!
General They used to be so loyal, so patriotic!
Sophia You are a murderer and a thief.
General Only when absolutely necessary!
Sophia And I hate your moustache!

The Villagers recoil, gasping with amazement

General My moustache!

Sophia It looks stupid!

General Stupid! My moustache looks stupid! (*To the Soldiers*) Well, don't just stand there gawping, arrest the bloody woman!

Major Company! By the right — forward ——

Ahmed (*stepping forward*) No, wait! Stop! This is wrong, what you do is wrong: her soup is a gift to us all.

General Out of the way, you filthy foreigner!

Ahmed No! I will not! If you arrest her, you must first arrest me!

General Stupid man! Very well — put him under arrest!

Hannah (*stepping forward*) Arrest him, and you must first arrest me!

Shamir (*stepping forward*) And if you arrest her, you must also arrest me.

Camilla And me.

Kausu And me.

One by one, all the Villagers step forward and say "And me." Then there is a pause

General This cannot be tolerated. All of you! If you value your lives, I advise you to return to your homes at once.

No-one moves

Hopeless fools. Would you lose your life for a bowl of soup?

Sophia Not soup. Stone soup, soup made from the fruits of the earth ...

Hannah — for us all ——

Ahmed — for everyone ——

Camilla — to enjoy and to share ——

Makomo — so that we all live together ——

Hannah — in peace and fellowship ——

Shamir — share it, share it with us ——

General *Me* share with *you*?

Makomo Why not?

General Why not? Share with my inferiors? Are you mad?

Shamir One world, one people, one pot — why not?

General Because there won't be enough, that's why not.
Hannah If we are wise, there is plenty.
General Not if there are to be extra helpings.
Hannah Then do without.
General Do without? Dear, oh, dear ... do without! (*He laughs*) Did you hear that, Mr North? We're to do without extra helpings. I should co-co.
Henry Er — yes — quite.
Hannah But why not? You eat too much, we eat too little. It will be better for us all.
General Don't be ridiculous. We've always had extra helpings. It's like ... like a tradition. Isn't that right, Mr North?
Henry Well, er, yes, yes, historically, I suppose by way of precedent ...
General And the more we want, the more we get. Survival of the fattest. That's the way it is and that's the way it's going to stay. Isn't that right, Mrs North?
Martha Damn right. I mean, after all, we do have big appetites.
General Big appetites and big bellies. That's why we need extra helpings. And that's why you wretches have to go without.
Hannah But how can that be fair!
General Fair? Fair! Of course it's not fair! Who said it had to be fair?
Hannah I do! I say it! I say it now!
General Silence!
Hannah And I will go on saying it! One world, one people, one pot!

The Villagers cheer and take up the chant

General Silence! (*He fires his pistol*) Since you seem so determined not to listen to reason, let me give you some advice You may be in the majority here, but never forget we have the guns. Now — I shall ask you one last time. Will you please stand aside?

No-one moves

Very well. Then you leave me no choice. Be it on your own heads. Company! By the right ... Present arms!

The Soldiers raise their rifles to shoot at the Villagers

   Company!

There is a drum roll

   At my command ——
Henry (*intervening*) General Mayhem, I must insist ——
General Prepare to fire.
Henry You might at least have the common decency to ——

The Soldiers release the safety catches of their rifles

General Take aim!
Henry Damn it, man — when we sold you those guns we didn't
   intend you to use them! And certainly not on innocent people!
General Innocent or guilty: who am I to judge? God can decide.
   Company!
Henry For God's sake, man, you can't shoot defenceless people,
   women and children!
General You think we are acting some fairy story, Mr North? This
   is not so special. It happens every day, only you rarely see it.
Henry This is outrageous! Martha, please, I'm furious, absolutely
   furious! We really have to do something!
Martha Yeah. Yeah, kinda looks that way, doesn't it? (*She swag-
   gers to confront the General*) OK soldier, listen up. Push has
   finally come to shove and you have just over-stepped the line. So
   let's just see you and your men back off and back down. Double-
   quick. Pronto. OK?
Henry God, Martha, I love it when you talk power.
Martha Are you hearing me?
General My hearing is perfect.
Martha I'll have you know that there cooking pot happens to be
   ours!
General Not any more.
Martha What?

General This cooking pot has been nationalized. It now belongs to
the people.
Martha Nationalized!
General (*to the soldiers*) Company ——
Martha Now just you listen here!
General — present arms!
Martha Do you realize how important and powerful and ——
General Take aim!
Martha Will you listen! Will you wait a goddamn -——
General Fire!

*Everyone breathes in very deeply. Tableau. There is silence except
for the cicadas singing in the dusk*

First Soldier (*sniffing the air*) Cor, that soup don't half smell
good ...
Second Soldier (*sniffing the air*) Yeah.
General I said "Fire!"
First Soldier You thinking what I'm thinking?
Second Soldier Yeah.
General Fire!
Major You can count me in.
General Are you deaf or stupid or what!
Third Soldier So what do we do about him?
General Fire!
First Soldier Well, not a lot of choice really.
Second Soldier Yeah.
General That's an order, you ugly cretins ——
First Soldier When the devil drives ——
Second Soldier Yeah ——
General Look, lads, please, be reasonable, you're making me look
a proper pillock.
First Soldier Sometimes it's necessary.
Second Soldier Yeah.
General Fire! Will you fire? Will you please, please fire!
First Soldier All right, then?

Second Soldier Yeah.
General Fire, damn you! Fire! Fire!

The soldiers fire at the General

Aaaagh! (*He dies*)

The Villagers cheer. Sophia solemnly stands over the body and holds up her hand for silence

Sophia Like you say — sometimes it is necessary. But, my friends, we must learn to live for causes, not die for them. And by killing this man you will not defeat what he represents. Besides, my story, it is about life, not death. So stand up, you sad and stupid man. Get up, I give you back your life.

The General miraculously recovers. The Villagers gasp

General What — what happened? Where am I? Who am I?

Everyone laughs

Sophia And so my story is almost at an end ...

The Villagers clap and sing

Villagers (*singing*) Why are we waiting
                            Why are we waiting
                            Oh, why are we ——
Sophia All right, all right!

The Villagers cheer

But first ... one last taste!

The Villagers groan. Sophia slurps the soup noisily. The Villagers grow tense and silent

Ah, perfect!

The Villagers cheer

Except for ——

The Villagers groan

— one final stir!

The Villagers cheer

And so, my friends — now, at last we can all eat!

The Villagers cheer. Sophia gestures to the Thin Girl, who comes forward holding her bowl. Sophia ladles stone soup and hands it back to the Girl

Here, my child ... You see, I did not forget.

The Thin Girl cups the stone soup in both hands and smiles

Hurry, take it to your brother.
Thin Girl Thank you. Thank you.

She runs off, calling back as she does

(*Off*) Thank you.
Sophia And now we all — we all have stone soup!

There are more cheers, then music — laughter — dance — carnival! Everyone forms a human chain, led by Sophia, to dance the conga, singing to their own "Bloop" accompaniment

Sophia I tell you, with stone soup we can feed the world!

They all encourage the audience to join in and join on ...

FURNITURE AND PROPERTY LIST

On stage: Stones

Off stage: Staff (**Sophia**)
Pot. *In it*: ladle (**Makomo and Villagers**)
Pieces of wood (**Camilla and Doreen**)
Cabbage (**Doreen**)
Salt (**Ahmed**)
Bowl (**Thin Girl**)
Turnip (**Child**)
Carrots (**Kausu**)
Salt beef and garlic (**Camilla**)
Chicken (**Henry**)
Proclamation (**Major Hazard**)
Rifles (**Soldiers**)

During Black-out p.8:
Set: Pile of firewood
Cardboard cut-out flames

LIGHTING PLOT

Property fittings required: nil

Bare stage with various interior and exterior settings suggested

To open: Bright exterior lighting fading to dusk throughout the play

Cue 1	**Sophia** spins the staff *Lights flash*	(Page 4)
Cue 2	**Makomo** runs in slow motion *Lights create impression of* *tropical jungle*	(Page 4)
Cue 3	**Sophia**: "Run like the wind!" *Lights create impression of city*	(Page 4)
Cue 4	**Makomo** stops running *Lights create impression of* *Henry North's house*	(Page 4)
Cue 5	Drumbeats build to a climax *Black-out*	(Page 8)
Cue 6	Drum-beats and African cries *Lights up on village*	(Page 8)
Cue 7	**Sophia:** "Oh, dear, dear, dear —— " *Lights flash*	(Page 18)
Cue 8	**Henry** hugs **Martha** *Lights focus on pot*	(Page 26)

EFFECTS PLOT

Throughout: Cicadas

Cue 1	**Sophia** raises her staff *Thunder*	(Page 3)
Cue 2	**Sophia**: "A great, big cooking pot!" *More thunder*	(Page 3)
Cue 3	**Makomo** runs in slow motion *Animal and bird cries*	(Page 4)
Cue 4	**Sophia**: "Run like the wind!" *Traffic noise and sirens*	(Page 4)
Cue 5	**Makomo** stops running *Traffic noise and sirens fade*	(Page 4)
Cue 6	**Makomo** mimes ringing doorbell *Doorbell*	(Page 4)
Cue 7	**Henry**: "Fantastic!" *Clock chimes eleven*	(Page 5)

Cue 8	**Makomo** looks thoughtful
	*Drum beats, building to a climax, then
	   silence and then more drums, with
	   African cries*
		(Page 8)

Cue 9	**Sophia:** " Feast the fire!" *Sound of fire crackling*	(Page 9)
Cue 10	**Martha** and **Henry** enter in car *Horn tooting and engine backfiring*	(Page 20)
Cue 11	**General**: "Company!" *Drum roll*	(Page 34)